INVASIVE SPECIES

NORWAY MAPLE

by Alicia Z. Klepeis

pogo

Ideas for Parents and Teachers

Pogo Books let children practice reading informational text while introducing them to nonfiction features such as headings, labels, sidebars, maps, and diagrams, as well as a table of contents, glossary, and index.

Carefully leveled text with a strong photo match offers early fluent readers the support they need to succeed.

Before Reading

- "Walk" through the book and point out the various nonfiction features. Ask the student what purpose each feature serves.
- Look at the glossary together. Read and discuss the words.

Read the Book

- Have the child read the book independently.
- Invite him or her to list questions that arise from reading.

After Reading

- Discuss the child's questions. Talk about how he or she might find answers to those questions.
- Prompt the child to think more. Ask: Norway maple tree seeds travel by wind. Why do you think this is a problem?

Pogo Books are published by Jump!
5357 Penn Avenue South
Minneapolis, MN 55419
www.jumplibrary.com

Copyright © 2023 Jump!
International copyright reserved in all countries. No part of this book may be reproduced in any form without written permission from the publisher.

Library of Congress Cataloging-in-Publication Data

Names: Klepeis, Alicia, 1971- author.
Title: Norway maple / by Alicia Z. Klepeis.
Description: Minneapolis, MN: Jump!, Inc., [2023]
Series: Invasive species | Includes index.
Audience: Ages 7-10
Identifiers: LCCN 2022029740 (print)
LCCN 2022029741 (ebook)
ISBN 9798885241137 (hardcover)
ISBN 9798885241144 (paperback)
ISBN 9798885241151 (ebook)
Subjects: LCSH: Norway maple—Juvenile literature.
Invasive plants—Juvenile literature.
Classification: LCC QK495.A17 K54 2023 (print)
LCC QK495.A17 (ebook)
DDC 538/.75—dc23/eng/20220721
LC record available at https://lccn.loc.gov/2022029740
LC ebook record available at https://lccn.loc.gov/2022029741

Editor: Eliza Leahy
Designer: Emma Bersie

Photo Credits: Sieboldianus/iStock, cover; C. Nass/Shutterstock, 1; Ihor Hvozdetskyi/Shutterstock, 3; Jan Martin Will/Dreamstime, 4; Niklas Gustafsson/Shutterstock, 5; Erkki Makkonen/Shutterstock, 6-7; blickwinkel/Alamy, 8-9, 11; Fotofermer/Shutterstock, 10, 23; Anmbph/Dreamstime, 12-13; Kazakov Maksim/Shutterstock, 13; Nigel Cattlin/Alamy, 14-15; ForestSeasons/Shutterstock, 16-17tl; fujilovers/Shutterstock, 16-17tr; Orchidpoet/iStock, 16-17bl; Studio Light and Shade/Shutterstock, 16-17br; thirawatana phaisalratana/Shutterstock, 18; Mainephotonut/Dreamstime, 19; GeorgePeters/iStock, 20-21.

Printed in the United States of America at Corporate Graphics in North Mankato, Minnesota.

TABLE OF CONTENTS

CHAPTER 1
Trees and Bees..4

CHAPTER 2
So Much Shade..10

CHAPTER 3
Going Local...18

ACTIVITIES & TOOLS
Try This!..22
Glossary..23
Index...24
To Learn More..24

CHAPTER 1

TREES AND BEES

What tree can grow 100 feet (30 meters) tall and produce thousands of seeds? It is a Norway maple! These trees have grayish-black bark. Their leaves are often green.

They grow small yellow-green flowers. The flowers have a lot of **nectar**. This draws in insects. Bees **pollinate** the trees. The trees grow fruit and seeds.

CHAPTER 1   5

This tree is **native** to western Asia and parts of Europe, including Norway. This is how it got its name.

Norway maples **adapt** well. They can live in both young and old forests. They often grow near sugar maples.

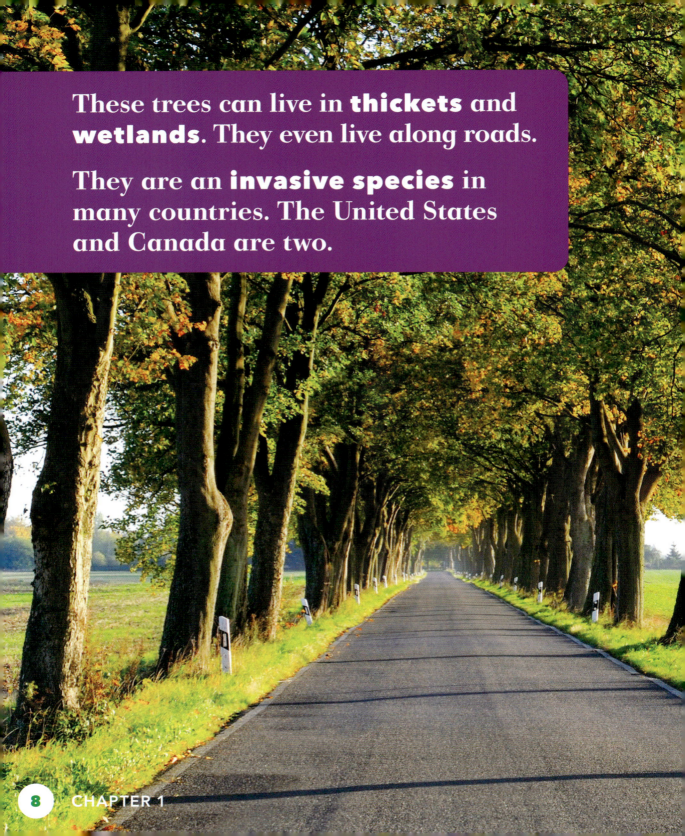

These trees can live in **thickets** and **wetlands**. They even live along roads.

They are an **invasive species** in many countries. The United States and Canada are two.

TAKE A LOOK!

Where have Norway maples been found in the United States and Canada? Take a look!

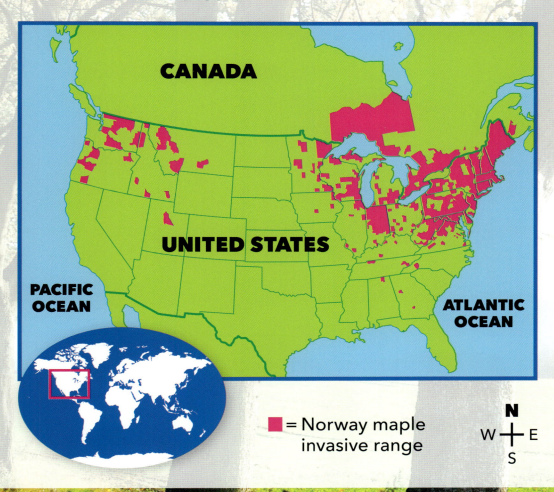

CHAPTER 2
SO MUCH SHADE

How did Norway maples get to North America? John Bartram was a **botanist**. He had **seedlings** sent from Europe in the mid-1700s. He sold them. Some people planted the tree for its beauty. Others liked how quickly it grew. By the late 1800s, it was popular throughout the United States.

seedling

People helped Norway maples spread by planting them. Cities planted the trees along streets. Why? They have a nice shape and size. They handle ice and snow well.

CHAPTER 2

Wind also spreads Norway maples. How? The trees' fruit has two wings. Each wing has a seed inside. The wind catches the wings. It carries the seeds to new areas. This leads to trees growing in areas they are not wanted.

DID YOU KNOW?

Norway maples usually live for about 150 years. That gives them a lot of time to spread their seeds.

wing

CHAPTER 2

As Norway maples grow taller, they get more sunlight. Their wide **crowns** create shade. Less sunlight reaches native plants below. The native plants have trouble growing. This means less food for animals that eat the plants.

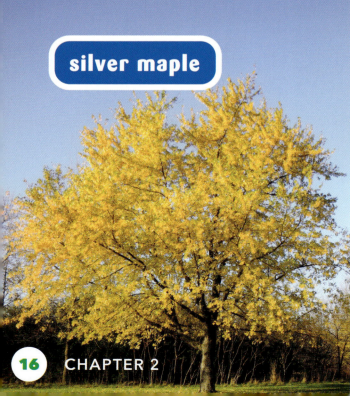

sugar maple

red maple

silver maple

tree tap

sap

There are many types of maple trees. Sugar, red, and silver maples are native to North America. These trees have trouble growing under Norway maples. If Norway maples keep spreading, there may be fewer sugar maples in the future.

DID YOU KNOW?

People collect **sap** from sugar maples to make maple syrup. It takes about 40 gallons (151 liters) of sap to make one gallon (3.8 L) of syrup. Sap from Norway maples is not good for making syrup.

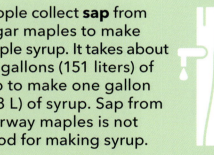

CHAPTER 2

CHAPTER 3
GOING LOCAL

Scientists learn about Norway maples. They study how native maple trees grow when nearby Norway maples are removed.

People work to stop the spread of Norway maples. How? They dig up young trees. They cut down big trees. Some use chemicals to kill the trees.

CHAPTER 3　19

How can you help? Planting native maple trees is a great way. The native wildlife will thank you!

DID YOU KNOW?

Some states **ban** the sale of Norway maples. Massachusetts and New Hampshire are two.

CHAPTER 3 21

ACTIVITIES & TOOLS

TRY THIS!

IDENTIFY LEAF SHAPES

Tree leaves come in many shapes. Create leaf rubbings and find out more about trees near you with this fun activity!

What You Need:
- leaves of different shapes and sizes
- tape
- clipboard
- paper
- crayon(s)
- computer and/or books

1. Collect several leaves of different shapes and sizes.
2. Make a tape loop. Attach it to the back of one leaf. Tape the leaf to the center of your clipboard.
3. Clip a piece of paper on the clipboard, on top of the leaf. Holding your crayon sideways, rub it over the leaf so that its outline and pattern show on the paper. Hint: It helps to remove the paper label from the crayon before rubbing with it.
4. Repeat Steps 2 and 3 with a new sheet of paper for each leaf.
5. Use a computer or books to find out what type of tree or plant the leaves came from. How do the leaves you found compare to those of a Norway maple?
6. Label your leaf rubbings with the information you found. Teach others about what you learned.

GLOSSARY

adapt: To change to fit a new situation.

ban: To officially forbid something or prevent someone from doing something.

botanist: A scientist who studies plants.

crowns: The upper parts of trees where their leaves are spread out.

invasive species: Any kind of living organism that is not native to a specific area.

native: Growing or living naturally in a particular area of the world.

nectar: A sweet liquid from flowers that bees gather and make into honey.

pollinate: To take pollen from the male part of a flower and put it on the female part of a flower so the plant can reproduce.

sap: The liquid that flows through a plant, carrying water and food from one part of the plant to another.

seedlings: Young plants that have grown from seeds.

thickets: Areas of plants, bushes, or small trees growing very close together.

wetlands: Areas of land where there is a lot of moisture in the soil.

ACTIVITIES & TOOLS

INDEX

adapt 6
animals 14, 21
ban 21
bark 4
Bartram, John 10
bees 5
botanist 10
chemicals 19
crowns 14
flowers 5
forests 6
fruit 5, 13
leaves 4
native 6, 14, 17, 18, 21
nectar 5
pollinate 5
range 9
sap 17
scientists 18
seedlings 10
seeds 4, 5, 13
shade 14
sugar maples 6, 17
wind 13

TO LEARN MORE

Finding more information is as easy as 1, 2, 3.
1. Go to www.factsurfer.com
2. Enter "Norwaymaple" into the search box.
3. Choose your book to see a list of websites.